W9-BDV-087

LIGHTNING BOLT BOOKS™

How Do Helicopters Work?

Jennifer Boothroyd

Lerner Publications Company
Minneapolis

For the H girls: Heather, Hannah, and Hayden —J.B.

Lerner Publications Company
A division of Lerner Publishing Group, Inc.
241 First Avenue North
Minneapolis, MN 55401 U.S.A.

Website address: www.lernerbooks.com

Library of Congress Cataloging-in-Publication Data

Boothroyd, Jennifer, 1972–
        How do helicopters work? / by Jennifer Boothroyd.
            p.   cm. — (Lightning bolt books™—how flight works)
        Includes index.
        ISBN 978–0–7613–8966–8 (lib. bdg. : alk. paper)
        1. Helicopters—Juvenile literature. I. Title.
    TL716.2.B66 2013
    387.7'3352—dc23   2012019112

Manufactured in the United States of America
1 — MG — 12/31/12

Table of Contents

What Is a Helicopter?

A helicopter is a kind of aircraft. Many parts work together to make it fly.

The main part of a helicopter is the fuselage. It's the body of the aircraft.

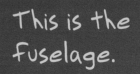
This is the fuselage.

The main rotor
is on top.
This part of
the helicopter
has blades
that spin.

These blades
spin to help the
helicopter fly.

The landing skids keep the body off the ground.

The tail boom connects the tail at the back. There's a small rotor on the tail.

The tail rotor spins on one side of the tail.

The cockpit is in the front. The pilot controls the helicopter from here.

Pilots use their hands and feet to fly a helicopter.

Flying a helicopter takes lots of skill.

Up, Up, and Away

Helicopters can lift off from almost anywhere. They need just a small, flat space.

It's time for takeoff!
Engines power the main rotor.
The blades spin fast.

The spinning blades create lift. **Lift is a force.** It makes things rise.

Lift works against gravity. Gravity pulls things down.

The blades also create torque. This force makes things turn.

Torque is pushing on the fuselage. The pilot works to keep it straight.

The tail rotor spins sideways. It works against the torque. This keeps the fuselage from spinning.

DANGER

DANGER

Flying

A helicopter can move in many directions.

The pilot tilts the main rotor. This creates thrust. Thrust is a force that moves an aircraft in the air.

This helicopter's main rotor is tilted forward.

RESCUE

Thrust makes the helicopter fly forward, backward, or sideways.

This rotor is tilted to one side.

The pilot pushes the foot pedals. This turns the tail of the helicopter left or right.

A helicopter can change directions quickly. This makes it perfect for doing certain jobs.

People film movies from helicopters.

Helicopters help firefighters put out forest fires too.

A helicopter can fly in one spot. This is called hovering.

Helicopters can carry heavy supplies.

A helicopter
can hover over
someone who
needs help.

Touchdown

This pilot slowly lowers her helicopter. She is getting close to the landing zone.

The helicopter hovers a few feet above the ground.

Then the pilot lowers it gently.

Touchdown!

Diagram of a Helicopter

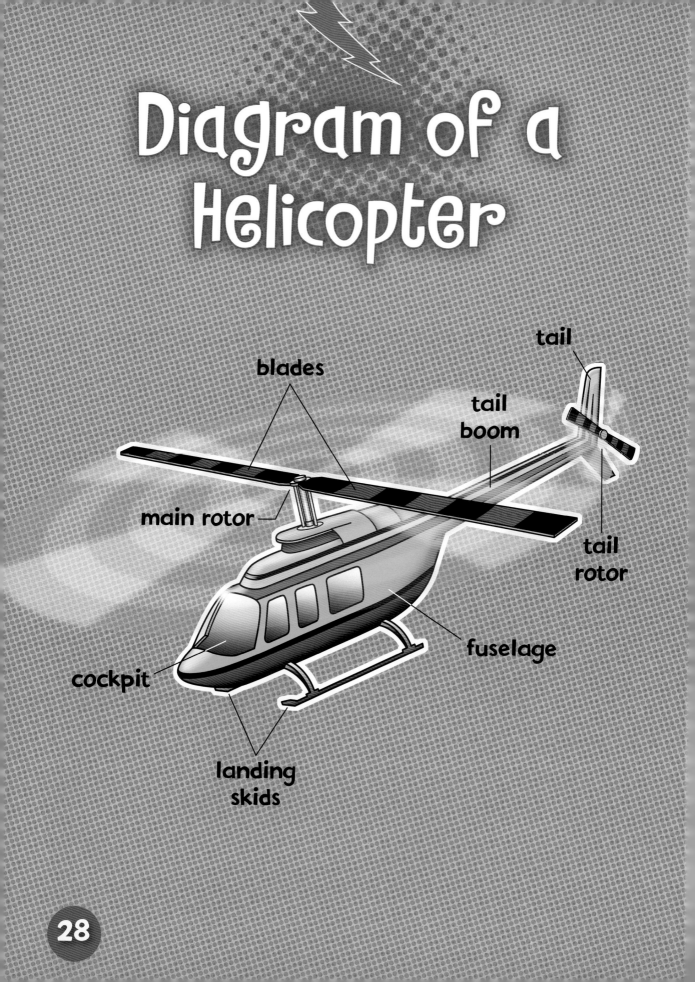

blades

tail

tail boom

main rotor

tail rotor

cockpit

fuselage

landing skids

Fun Facts

- A helicopter has three main controls. The collective lever moves the helicopter up and down. The foot pedals turn it left and right. The cyclic stick moves it forward, backward, and sideways.

- Leonardo da Vinci drew flying machines more than five hundred years ago. The idea for a helicopter may have come from his drawings.

- Igor Sikorsky invented the first working helicopter in the 1930s.

- U.S. emergency rescue helicopters carry about fifteen thousand patients to hospitals each year.

- The U.S. president takes short trips in the Marine One helicopter.

Glossary

aircraft: a vehicle that travels in the air

hover: to stay in one place in the air

lift: a force that pushes objects up in the air

rotor: blades that spin on a helicopter

thrust: a force that moves an aircraft in the air

torque: a force that makes things turn

Further Reading

Bodden, Valerie. *Helicopters.* Mankato, MN: Creative Education, 2012.

Hanson, Anders. *Let's Go by Helicopter.* Edina, MN: Abdo, 2008.

Helicopter Hotspot
http://www.firemansamonline.com/usa/Games/submenu/rescues/helicopter_hotspot/index.asp

How Helicopters Work
http://videos.howstuffworks.com/howstuffworks/4728-how-helicopters-work-video.htm

Newton's Apple: Helicopters
http://www.newtonsapple.tv/video_only.php?id=3052

Zuehlke, Jeffrey. *Helicopters on the Move.* Minneapolis: Lerner Publications Company, 2011.

Index

Photo Acknowledgments

The images in this book are used with the permission of: © Image Source/Getty Images, p. 1; © Peter Lovas/Dreamstime.com, p. 2; © Zagor/Dreamstime.com, p. 4; © Ivan Cholakov/Dreamstime.com, pp. 5, 8; © Manw Olste/Dreamstime.com, p. 6; © Dani3315/Dreamstime.com, p. 7; © Henn Photography/Cultura/Getty Images, p. 9; © Paul Souders/CORBIS, p. 10; © Ashley Cooper/CORBIS, p. 11; © Travel Ink/Gallo Images/Getty Images, p. 12; © Mark Hannaford/AWL Images/Getty Images, p. 13; © imagebroker.net/SuperStock, p. 14; © Misscanon/Dreamstime.com, p. 15; © Lorenzo Puricelli/Vetta/Getty Images, p. 16; © Bena Elisseeva/Dreamstime.com, p. 17; © Colette6/Dreamstime.com, p. 18; © Bridget Webber/Photodisc/Getty Images, p. 19; © Stocktrek/Digital Vision/Getty Images, p. 20; © Tony Arruza/CORBIS, p. 21; © Philip Wallick/CORBIS/Glow Images, p. 22; © Jared Hobbs/All Canada Photos/SuperStock, p. 23; © Ashley Cooper Pics/Alamy, p. 24; © Joanne Rathe/The Boston Globe via Getty Images, p. 25; © Claver Carroll/Photolibrary/Getty Images, p. 26; © George Stienmetz/CORBIS, p. 27; © Laura Westlund/Independent Picture Service, p. 28; © Steven Dahlman/SuperStock, p. 30; © iStockphoto.com/Dmitry Mordvintsev, p. 31.

Front cover: © iStockphoto.com/Terry North.

Main body text set in Johann Light 30/36.